Prayers *for* Public Worship

Advent and the Season of Christmas

David Adam
Nick Fawcett
Susan Sayers
Ray Simpso

kevin mayhew

kevin mayhew

First published in Great Britain in 2012 by Kevin Mayhew Ltd
Buxhall, Stowmarket, Suffolk IP14 3BW
Tel: +44 (0) 1449 737978 Fax: +44 (0) 1449 737834
E-mail: info@kevinmayhewltd.com

www.kevinmayhew.com

9 8 7 6 5 4 3 2 1 0

ISBN 978 1 84867 5261
Catalogue No. 1501358

Cover design by Rob Mortonson
© Images used under licence from Shutterstock Inc.
Typeset by Richard Weaver

Printed and bound in Great Britain

Contents

About the authors

DAVID ADAM was the Vicar of Lindisfarne, off the Northumbrian coast, for thirteen years until he retired in March 2003. His work involved ministering to thousands of pilgrims and other visitors. He is the author of many inspiring books on spirituality and prayer, and his Celtic writings have rekindled a keen interest in our Christian heritage.

NICK FAWCETT was brought up in Southend-on-Sea, Essex, and trained for the Baptist ministry at Bristol and Oxford, before serving churches in Lancashire and Cheltenham. He subsequently spent three years as a chaplain with the Christian movement Toc H, before focusing on writing and editing, which he continues with today, despite wrestling with cancer. He lives with his wife, Deborah, and two children – Samuel and Kate – in Wellington, Somerset, worshipping at the local Anglican church. A keen walker, he delights in the beauty of the Somerset and Devon countryside around his home, his numerous books owing much to the inspiration he unfailingly finds there.

SUSAN SAYERS is the author of many popular resource books for the church. Through the conferences and workshops she is invited to lead, she has been privileged to share in the worship of many different traditions and cultures. A teacher by profession, she was ordained a priest in the Anglican Church and, before her retirement, her work was divided between the parish of Westcliff-on-Sea, the local women's prison, writing, training days and retreats.

RAY SIMPSON is a Celtic new monastic for tomorrow's world, a lecturer, consultant, liturgist, and author of some 30 books. He is the founding guardian of the international Community of Aidan and Hilda and the pioneer of its e-studies programmes. He is an ordained member of the Christian church and lives on the Holy Island of Lindisfarne. His website is www.raysimpson.org

215 Thank you, heavenly Father,
for the extraordinary love you show for us
in entering our world
through the natural channel of birth.   *Susan Sayers*

216 Incarnate God,
we love you and we need you.
We give thanks and praise
for your involvement in our lives.   *Susan Sayers*

217 Loving Lord,
though we cannot see you,
your love surrounds us.
We bring to mind the risks you were prepared to take
in becoming one of us out of love for us,
and we offer you our thanks and praise.   *Susan Sayers*

218 Jesus,
the best present
I can give you
is myself!   *Susan Sayers*

219 Thank you, Lord God,
for coming to save us.   *Susan Sayers*

220 Jesus, born in a stable,
make here your home.
Jesus, born of a peasant girl,
make here your home.
Jesus, searched for by wise seekers,
make here your home.
Jesus, reared at a carpenter's bench,
make here your home.
Jesus, risen from the wintry ground of death,
make here your home.   *Ray Simpson*

221 Homemaker God,
who made yourself at home in a cowshed,
come to all who are sleeping rough.
May the light of the Bethlehem family
be a light for the homeless in our world.   *Ray Simpson*

222   May we journey with you,
      Jesus, Mary and Joseph,
      to your birthplace at Bethlehem,
      firm in the faith,
      loyal to the truth,
      obedient to your Father's will
      along the path that leads to life.   *Ray Simpson*

223   Universal Child,
      we will welcome you when you call.
      We will open the long-shut parts of our lives.
      We will become young again with you.   *Ray Simpson*

224   Babe of heaven, Defenceless Love,
      you had to travel far from your home.
      Strengthen us on our pilgrimage of trust on Earth.
      King of Glory, you accepted such humbling;
      clothe us with the garments of humility.
      Your birth shows us the simplicity of the Father's love;
      keep us in the simplicity of that love.
      Your coming shows us the wonder of being human;
      help us to cherish every human life.

      Based on a prayer of George Appleton   *Ray Simpson*

225   Now is born Christ the king of greatness.
      Glow to him stars and streets;
      glow to him churches and trees.   *Ray Simpson*

226   Thank you for the holy family,
      Mary, Joseph and the others.
      May families reflect their dedication to put your will first;
      may purity, love and trust grow strong in our households.

                            Ray Simpson

227   Thank you for the prophetess Anna
      who, honed in daily attunement to you
      in the offering of praise,
      discerned your presence
      in an ordinary but significant moment.

Take our senses, hone our intuition,
steep us in the disciplines of the Spirit,
that we may see your hand at work
in the events of today and tomorrow. *Ray Simpson*

228 Thank you for the sanctuaries of Egypt
that were offered to the holy family,
for their acquaintance with God-honourers
of another land and religion,
for the hermits and holy people of the deserts.
We pray for God-honourers
who seek to welcome your servants
in Egypt, in Muslim lands and everywhere;
for refugees, for hermits and others who pattern
an alternative way to that of our acquisitive society.

Ray Simpson

229 Thank you for the home in Nazareth,
and for the boy Jesus
growing in skills of carpentry
and in the confidence of puberty.
We pray for young people who are confused,
deskilled, orphaned,
and who know neither themselves nor their calling:
may they find affirming adults to be alongside them.

Ray Simpson

230 Thank you that even at the death of Jesus,
the holy family grew through the adoption of John
into Mary's family.
We pray for those who have died,
and for those who face loss of life or limb or hope.
May the healing light of Christ shine upon them,
and may they come to know that there is
a family more wonderful than they have ever known.

Ray Simpson

231 Lord of time and eternity,
prepare our minds to celebrate with faith
your birth on Earth.

Fill our hearts with wonder
as we recall the precious moment
when you were born as our brother. *Ray Simpson*

232 May every lone parent and child
be cherished as Mary cherished you.
May those who are out in the cold
find a stable place as warm as yours.
May those who work on the land
be as responsive to your presence as were the shepherds.
Ray Simpson

233 Let the cares of the past grow dim,
let the skies and our hearts grow clear,
until the Son of God comes striding towards us
walking on this Earth. *Ray Simpson*

234 Jesus, proclaimed by angels;
light up our darkness.
Jesus, worshipped by shepherds;
light up our darkness.
Jesus, adored by wise men;
light up our darkness.
Jesus, God who is with us now;
light up our darkness. *Ray Simpson*

235 Jesus, you are the glory of eternity shining among us,
the tenderness of God here with us now.
Jesus, you are the Healing Person, the pattern of goodness,
fulfilling among us the highest human hopes.
Jesus, you are the champion of the weak,
the counsellor of the despairing,
the brother of us all, who knows our every need.
Jesus, you are the splendour of the Father, the Son of Mary,
our Bridge between Earth and the world beyond.
Ray Simpson

236 Angels' Lord, who for nine months
was hidden in love's furnace, Mary's womb –
you who stole down to Earth, humbler than all –
take us to yourself, and make us like you. *Ray Simpson*

237   The Earth gave you a cave,
the skies gave you a star,
the angels gave you a song;
may we give you our love.

Based on an Orthodox prayer   *Ray Simpson*

238   The love that Mary gave her Son
may we give to the world;
the love that you give us through your Son
may we give back to you.   *Ray Simpson*

239   Son of the elements, Son of the heavens,
Son of the moon, Son of the sun,
Son of Mary of the God-mind,
Son of God, firstborn of all creation,
dwell with us today.   *Ray Simpson*

240   Jesus Christ, Son of glory,
who for love comes among us,
bless to us this day of joy.
Open to us heaven's generous gates.
Strengthen our hope.
Revive our tired souls
till we sing the joys of your glory
with all the angels of heaven.
Hold also those who are sleeping rough,
those who feel shut out of society,
those who are cold and hungry,
and these we name before you now.   *Ray Simpson*

241   Bless, O Lord, this Christmas tree,
all that goes on to it
and all that goes on around it.
May the needles that point upwards
lead us to worship the Creator
who came from heaven to be born as a child.

May the needles that fall to the ground
remind us of the needs of the poor
and those at the bottom of the social pile.
May the decorations that brighten this dark season
prompt us to celebrate it with thoughtfulness and joy.

Ray Simpson

242   Child of Glory, Child of Mary,
at your birth you were proclaimed the Prince of Peace.
You came to remove the wall
that divides one people from another;
may walls of hostility and fear come tumbling down.

Ray Simpson

243   O Saviour Christ,
you existed before the world began.
You came to save us and we are witnesses of your goodness.
You became a tiny child in a cot
showing us the simplicity of our parents' love.
You chose Mary as your mother
and raised all motherhood to a divine vocation.
May all mothers be bearers of life and grace
to their husbands, their children
and to all who come to their homes.   *Ray Simpson*

244   Today, O Lord,
as we contemplate Mary and Joseph,
may we live in the wonder of your divine conceiving;
may we live in the wonder of our divine receiving.

Ray Simpson

245   Child of Glory, Child of Mary,
born in the stable,
King of all.
You came to our wasteland,
in our place suffered,
come to us now with your call.   *Ray Simpson*

246　Birther, Father, Mother of the cosmos,
　　　breathing through all creation,
　　　breathing your life through a woman's womb
　　　into a human form:
　　　bring new birth to us who gather
　　　at this time of the Birth.
　　　Bring birth to our nation,
　　　to this ailing, ageing world,
　　　and bring to birth in us,
　　　who are your people,
　　　the new creation
　　　which we stand on tiptoe to see.　　　*Ray Simpson*

247　God bless to us this year,
　　　never vouchsafed to us before.
　　　It is to bless your own presence
　　　that you have given us this moment, O Lord.
　　　Bless to us our eyes
　　　and everything they shall see.
　　　Bless to us our neighbours;
　　　may our neighbours be a blessing to us.
　　　Bless to us our households
　　　and all our dear ones.
　　　Bless to us our work
　　　and all that belongs to our provision.
　　　Give to us clean hearts
　　　that we may not need to hide from you
　　　one moment of this new year.　　　*Ray Simpson*

248　Lord of the years,
　　　we will ring out the old year,
　　　the lust to gain,
　　　the craze to destroy,
　　　we will ring in the new year,
　　　the joy of being,
　　　the will to transform.　　　*Ray Simpson*

249   God of the years,
      at the gate of the year we put our hands in yours.
      As the old tide recedes,
      may we plant your footsteps in fresh sands.
      May we travel with less baggage and more wisdom
      and learn from you how our journey should be.

Ray Simpson

250   Lord of the year behind us,
      Lord of the year before us,
      as Mary and Joseph named Jesus in the temple,
      may we name him in our hearts,
      receive him in this Eucharist
      and journey with him through this year.   *Ray Simpson*

251   Bless to us this time of threshold,
      when we pass from the old to the new.
      Bless to us this bread,
      made from grains of wheat that pass away,
      that it may become for us
      the food that nurtures new life.
      Bless to us this wine,
      made from grapes that pass away,
      that it may become for us
      the drink of heaven's ever-renewing life.   *Ray Simpson*

252   Lord, with joy and for love of you
      we commit ourselves to seek and do
      your perfect will in this coming year.
      We are no longer our own but yours.
      Put us to what you will;
      place us with whom you will;
      let us be put to work for you or put aside for you;
      let us be full, let us be empty;
      let us have all things, let us have nothing.
      We freely and with all our heart
      give you all things for you to use.
      May we walk with you through this year
      in unity with our fellow Christians,

feeding upon your Word,
honouring all people,
serving our neighbour,
responsive to the leading of your Holy Spirit.
Based on words from The Methodist Covenant Service

Ray Simpson

253   You have given your all to us.
May this food and drink of angels
fortify us to give our all to you
in all whom we shall meet
and in all that we shall do
throughout the coming year.   *Ray Simpson*

254   Holy Father, Holy Jesus, Holy Guide,
be a smooth way before you,
a guiding star above you,
a keen eye behind you;
this day, this year, for ever.   *Ray Simpson*

Epiphany

255   God, who by the leading of a star
       brought the wise men to the Christ child,
       guide our journey and our seeking,
       until we glimpse his glory,
       and rejoice in his presence.   *David Adam*

256   God, by the leading of a star
       you brought the wise men to come before Jesus.
       In our seeking lead us to know you,
       to love you and to worship you
       this day and always.   *David Adam*

257   God, who by the shining of a star
       brought the wise men to see the Christ and to offer gifts,
       may we know his presence today
       and offer him our love and our lives.   *David Adam*

258   Blessed are you, Lord our God,
       who by the leading of a star
       brought seekers from other nations
       to bow before the Christ child.
       As they offered their gifts and their lives,
       may we offer ourselves to you in love and adoration,
       for you are the giver of life and life eternal.   *David Adam*

259   God, lighten our journey and direct our way.
       As we seek your presence and long for you,
       lead us until we come before the Child of Mary:
       guide us until we bow in love and adoration.
       As we remember the journeying of the wise men,
       and the offering of their gifts,
       help us to give our hearts to Christ,
       and to spend our lives in his service.   *David Adam*

260   We rejoice with Mary and Joseph,
       with the shepherds and the angels,
       with the wise men,
       with the Church in heaven and on earth.
       We commend ourselves, all peoples and the whole world
       to your unfailing love.   *David Adam*

261   We come before the Christ child,
      we kneel before the infant,
      we adore with the shepherds,
      we worship with the wise men,
      we love him with Mary and Joseph,
      we wonder at the 'Word made flesh',
      we bow before the mystery.
      We sing glory to God with the angels.
      We will travel this day rejoicing,
      glorifying and praising God.   *David Adam*

262   Sovereign God,
      we are reminded today of the journey of the magi:
      of how they stepped out into the unknown,
      persevering despite adversity,
      searching diligently until their quest was rewarded.
      We come today, seeking in our turn:
      looking to learn from their experience,
      to worship the one before whom they knelt in homage,
      to understand what his birth, life, death and resurrection
      mean for us.
      Help us to discover each day a little more of your love,
      and to discern more of your gracious purpose,
      so that we may offer our lives to you,
      in joyful praise
      and glad thanksgiving
      through Jesus Christ our Lord.   *Nick Fawcett*

263   Lord Jesus Christ,
      Light of the World,
      you shine in our hearts,
      banishing all that obscures your goodness
      and darkens our lives.
      Illuminate this time of worship,
      so that in every part it will draw us closer to you,
      revealing more of your purpose
      and unfolding more of your grace.
      Come to us
      as we come now to you,

and flood our lives with the radiance of your love
so that it may shine not just in us
but also through us –
a light set upon a hill.   *Nick Fawcett*

264   Lord Jesus Christ,
      hope of your people,
      hope of your world,
      touch now our lives as we gather before you.
      Shine in our hearts,
      illumine our minds
      and light up our spirits,
      so that we will grasp more clearly
      the hope you give us:
      the assurance of your love
      and the joy of life in all its fullness,
      giving you praise and worship.   *Nick Fawcett*

265   Gracious God,
      remind us again as we worship you of how much you love us
      and how much you are willing to do for our sakes.
      Teach us to appreciate the full extent of your devotion
      and to respond by consecrating our lives to Christ,
      so that his grace may flow through us,
      leading us out of darkness into his marvellous light.
      Shine upon us, within us and through us,
      and make us new
      for we ask it in his name.   *Nick Fawcett*

266   Sovereign God,
      without your light in our lives we walk in darkness,
      denied the joy, peace, hope, strength and guidance
      that you alone can give.
      So we ask, through this time of worship,
      that the light of Christ might break yet more fully into
      our hearts
      and shine more brightly through our lives,
      to your glory.   *Nick Fawcett*

267   Thank you, Lord,
for the new day you bring through the rising of your Son –
the new beginnings, new life,
you daily make possible through him.
Thank you for your promise that,
however deep the darkness may seem,
light will dawn again,
shining in our hearts for evermore.   *Nick Fawcett*

268   Thank you, Lord,
for your light,
guiding to Bethlehem, shining on the mountain,
pouring from the empty tomb and sparkling in our hearts.
Thank you for the knowledge that,
whatever life brings,
you will give light to our path,
this and every day.   *Nick Fawcett*

269   Lord Jesus Christ,
Light of the world,
shine on us,
shine in us,
shine through us,
and so bring honour to your name.   *Nick Fawcett*

270   God of life,
may the promise of the sunrise be echoed in our minds,
the warmth of the midday sun flow into our hearts
and the peace of the sunset touch our souls;
and, when life seems dark,
teach us to remember that still you are with us
and that we will again see your light.   *Nick Fawcett*

271   Eternal God,
when life seems a puzzle
and faith itself can make no sense of it,
lead us forward out of darkness into light,
out of confusion into certainty,
out of the storm into tranquillity.
Put our minds at rest and our spirits at peace,
through Jesus Christ our Lord.   *Nick Fawcett*

272   God of light,
      be with us in our darkness,
      until night passes and your light breaks through.

Nick Fawcett

273   Gracious God,
      even when all seems dark,
      teach us that your light will continue to shine. *Nick Fawcett*

274   Lord Jesus Christ,
      like the wise men following your birth,
      teach us to search for you until we come to faith,
      and then to go on searching just as eagerly and
      whole-heartedly
      to discover more of your will and purpose for our lives.
      Continue to surprise us with the wonder of your love
      and the awesomeness of your grace,
      so that we may know you and love you better each day,
      to the glory of your name.   *Nick Fawcett*

275   Lord Jesus Christ,
      you have told us to seek and we shall find.
      Yet that search is not always easy.
      As we look for meaning in our lives,
      there is so much that puzzles and perplexes.
      The more we discover,
      the more we realise how little we have understood.
      Give us the determination of the wise men to keep
      on looking,
      despite all that obscures you,
      until at last we find our perseverance rewarded
      and, glimpsing your glory,
      we kneel before you in joyful worship.   *Nick Fawcett*

276   Gracious God,
      such is your love for us that you go on calling
      however long it takes for us to respond,
      and you go on leading
      however tortuous our journey of faith may be.

We may put off a decision,
keep you at arm's length –
still you are there to guide,
striving to draw us to yourself.
We may encounter obstacles that impede our progress,
that lead us astray or that obscure the truth,
yet always you are there to set us back on the way.
Teach us that your love will never let us go,
and so help us to make our response
and to bring our lives to you in joyful homage,
knowing that you will continue to lead us until our
journey's end,
through Jesus Christ our Lord. *Nick Fawcett*

277   The night is turning to day,
darkness is turning to light –
it is time to wake from our sleep.
Wherever there is sorrow, fear, need or hurt,
let us reach out in the name of Christ,
and may his joy and peace,
healing and compassion,
dawn through us, until morning has broken
and the day of his kingdom is here. *Nick Fawcett*

278   Lord Jesus Christ,
may the flame of faith burn brightly within us,
and your light shine in our hearts,
so that we, in turn, may bring light to others,
to the glory of your name. *Nick Fawcett*

279   We thank you, God, for including us
in the plan of salvation.
We offer ourselves to you
and pray that we may be made worthy
of our calling. *Susan Sayers*

280   Lord, guide our hearts;
may they always be ready
to travel in your way
and in your direction. *Susan Sayers*

281   Lord, in those times in our lives
where we find our way
tedious, lonely or frightening;
when we have lost our way
and do not know what to do for the best,
give us courage and patience
to trust in you and keep walking your path.   *Susan Sayers*

282   Lord God, the world lurches from crisis to crisis,
and there is much misleading and misdirecting;
help us recover the natural sense
of what is right and just, honest and good,
so that our hearts are inclined
to hear the voice of your leading and respond to it.
   Susan Sayers

283   We pray that the light of God
will shine in all the dark corners of the Church,
and set us free from prejudice,
small-mindedness and hypocrisy;
that as members of the Body of Christ
we can move freely through the power of God
wherever we are called to go,
available and active in God's service.   *Susan Sayers*

284   Lord of light
we pray that our world may be lit
by your light in the darkness
to bring us freedom and hope,
recognition and respect,
and in all conflicts positive ways forward.   *Susan Sayers*

285   Holy God, we thank you
for making yourself known to us
in the many blessings of life,
and most of all in
the person of Jesus, the Christ.   *Susan Sayers*

286 We thank you, God,
     for all those who brought
     the good news of Jesus to us,
     and all who nourish our faith today.
     May we work as people of God
     in unity and openness
     for the coming of your kingdom.   *Susan Sayers*

287 We thank you, God,
     that salvation is for all people,
     and pray for a just and accepting world
     where none is rejected, despised
     or treated with contempt.   *Susan Sayers*

288 We give you thanks for all that points us
     towards the beauty of your love,
     and draws us closer to you.
     Direct us, Lord,
     and we will follow.   *Susan Sayers*

289 Light of the world,
     shine in our darkness.
     Make us always
     ready to travel
     in your way
     and in your direction.   *Susan Sayers*

290 God with us,
     as we live through conflicts
     and struggle with our identity,
     we long for the courage
     to always acknowledge you,
     the true and living God.   *Susan Sayers*

291 This is a prayer the wise men might have said. We have all
     been invited to find Jesus as well, so we can say it with them:

     Thank you, Jesus,
     for inviting me
     to come and look for you.
     I am glad I have found you!   *Susan Sayers*

292   *Gold*

The wise men brought gold to Jesus.
Jesus, we bring you the gold of our obedience.
Help us to live as you want us to.

Frankincense

The wise men brought frankincense to Jesus.
Jesus, we bring you the incense of our worship.
You are God and we worship you.

Myrrh

The wise men brought myrrh to Jesus.
Jesus, we bring you the myrrh of the world's sadness.
Help us to look after one another better.   *Susan Sayers*

293   Jesus, I believe and trust
that you are God's Son,
the promised Saviour,
the Christ, the Messiah of God.   *Susan Sayers*

294   Jesus, we can't see God,
but you show us what God is like.
Help us to be kind and loving
as you are kind and loving.   *Susan Sayers*

295   We welcome your light that glints in the rising sun.
We welcome the light that dawns through your only Son.
We welcome your light that gleams through growing earth.
We welcome the light that you kindle in our souls.

    Ray Simpson

296   The magi searched for an infant king;
Christ, lead us into your presence.
They offered incense as their prayer;
Christ, we bow in awe before you.
Myrrh they gave to mourn your death;
Christ, to you we pour out our suffering love.   *Ray Simpson*

297 Purify our lives like gold
   that we may be royal priests to you.
   Sanctify our hearts like incense
   that we may be adorers of your presence.
   Beautify our hearts like myrrh
   that we may be your fragrance on Earth. *Ray Simpson*

298 May your presence draw people across the world
   and reveal your mother heart of compassion.
   Pour into the empty cups of the world
   the beauty and blessings of Christ
   and gather together your children. *Ray Simpson*

299 You who became poor to make many rich:
   transform our dullness with radiant light;
   transform our drabness with vibrant joy;
   transform our shallowness with deepening wisdom;
   transform our suffering with growing trust. *Ray Simpson*

300 Infant Jesus,
   truly God, truly human,
   truly infinite, truly frail,
   your greatness holds the universe;
   your face attracts our hearts;
   your goodness beckons all that is good in us;
   your wisdom searches us;
   your truth reshapes us;
   your generosity enriches our poverty;
   your hand fills us with blessings;
   your mercy brings forgiveness.
   Your glory fills the world. *Ray Simpson*

301 O Christ, you entered the stream of human life:
   immerse us in the divine life.
   Immerse us in the waters that cleanse.
   Immerse us in the waters that overwhelm evil.
   Immerse us in the waters of creativity.
   Immerse us in the waters of life everlasting. *Ray Simpson*

302 Christ, splendour of the Father's glory,
     sustaining all the worlds by your Word of power,
     renew your presence in our lives.
     Christ, child of Mary, rich in wisdom,
     Prince of Peace, God with us,
     renew your presence in our homes.
     Christ, begotten of the Father before time,
     born at Bethlehem in time,
     renew your presence in your Church.
     Christ, truly God, truly human,
     fulfilling the desires of the peoples,
     renew your presence in the people.   *Ray Simpson*

303 Great God,
     in creation you commanded the light
     to shine out of darkness.
     As the season of darkness recedes
     may the incoming light be to us the true Light
     in whose presence no unworthy thought,
     no deed of shame,
     may stubbornly remain.   *Ray Simpson*

304 Shed light upon our brow
     and on what we grow.
     Shed light upon our cheek
     and on what we seek.
     Shed light upon the seeds
     and on our deeds.   *Ray Simpson*

305 May you be
     lit by the glory of God,
     drawn by the light of God,
     warmed by the fire of God.

     After Brian Frost   *Ray Simpson*

This book brings together over 300 beautiful prayers for
Advent and the Season of Christmas, written by four of
the best-loved and most distinguished Christian writers:

David Adam
Nick Fawcett
Susan Sayers
Ray Simpson

It is an invaluable resource for all those who prepare
public worship.

kevin
mayhew

Product Code 1501358

ISBN 978-1-84867-526-1

9 781848 675261

MIX
Paper from
responsible sources
FSC® C104323

KT-476-431

See every Kevin Mayhew book in print at www.kevinmayhew.com

Advent

First Sunday of Advent

1 Come, my Lord,
   my light, my way;
   come, my lantern,
   night and day;
   come, healer,
   make me whole.
   Come, my Saviour,
   protect my soul;
   come, my King,
   enter my heart;
   come, Prince of Peace,
   and never depart.   *David Adam*

2 Awaken us, O God, to your coming.
   Open our eyes that we may see you.
   Open our ears that we may hear you.
   Open our lips that we may talk about you.
   Touch our hearts that we may love you.
   Come, Lord, come among us.   *David Adam*

3 Lord, as you come to your Church,
   help us to reveal your glory.
   Grant that we may show your grace
   and your goodness in our lives.
   We thank you for the grace and goodness
   revealed in Jesus Christ
   and that we are enriched in him.   *David Adam*

4 He comes to you today as he came yesterday.
   He will come again tomorrow, as he came today.
   He comes to you always.
   Welcome him. Say, 'Come, Lord Jesus.'   *David Adam*

5 Come, Lord.
   You were broken on the cross to make us whole.
   Be with all who are suffering at this time.
   Come as light to those who walk in darkness,
   the despairing and the despondent.

Come as joy to all who have lost confidence
and to all who are depressed.
Come as hope to all who are ill
and fearful of their future.   *David Adam*

6   Rejoice, for Christ comes: he is a light in our darkness.
He comes as of old, to those on the edge of a new day,
to those fearful and wanting to turn back,
to those with hard decisions to make,
to those who have been long in the desert. He comes.
Rejoice, for Christ comes: he is a light in our darkness.
                                                David Adam

7   He comes to all who are being challenged,
to those who are being overwhelmed,
to those who are facing a fiery ordeal,
to those longing for freedom,
to all who are seeking a better world. He comes.
Rejoice, for Christ comes: he is a light in our darkness.
                                                David Adam

8   He comes to those who live in simplicity,
to those who thirst for justice,
to those who hunger for righteousness,
to those who repent of their sins,
to those who turn away from evil. He comes.
Rejoice, for Christ comes: he is a light in our darkness.
                                                David Adam

9   He comes to those who seek to do his will,
who wait upon his word;
to all who magnify his name,
to all who rejoice in him as Saviour,
to each of us in our homes. He comes.
Rejoice, for Christ comes: he is a light in our darkness.
                                                David Adam

10   He comes to ordinary working people,
     to all who are awake and alert,
     to those going about their daily work,
     to those who care for his creation,
     to the humble and the meek. He comes.
     Rejoice, for Christ comes: he is a light in our darkness.

David Adam

11   He comes to the seekers and the searchers,
     to all who will not be put off,
     to those who travel in darkness,
     to those not sure of their journey,
     to everyone who offers their heart to him. He comes.
     Rejoice, for Christ comes: he is a light in our darkness.

David Adam

First week of Advent

12   Lord, you tell us to look forward,
     anticipating the dawn of your kingdom.
     We've no idea when that shall be or what it will mean,
     but, however long the wait,
     teach us to look forward expectantly,
     assured that the day will come:
     a day that will transform not only our lives,
     but the whole world, for ever.   *Nick Fawcett*

13   Though we speak of your coming again, Lord,
     your return to establish your kingdom,
     it's hard to anticipate it meaningfully,
     and part of us doesn't want to,
     for you've given so much here and now that's good,
     and it would seem wrong to overlook this life
     through dwelling on the next.
     Yet don't let us lose altogether our sense of expectation;
     that conviction that one day your will shall be done –
     sorrow overcome,
     evils righted,
     love triumphant,
     death itself destroyed.   *Nick Fawcett*

14   It's hard to keep faith that your kingdom will come, Lord,
for so much in the world seems to deny your love
and frustrate your will.
However hard it may be, though,
help us to trust in your promises,
daring to believe that despite everything that conspires
against it,
the day will come when your love finally triumphs over all.

Nick Fawcett

15   We like to think we're ready, Lord –
to serve you,
to respond to your call, and to welcome you when you
come again –
but too often our discipleship flatters to deceive,
promising much yet delivering little.
Come, Lord, and fill us afresh,
that we may live and work for you.   *Nick Fawcett*

16   Teach us, Lord, that you are a God who repeatedly turns
the tables;
the way of Christ,
if taken seriously,
challenging the assumptions of this world
and upsetting the status quo.
Teach us that, though it may not sometimes seem like it,
you will finally correct injustice,
overcome evil and undo wrongs,
in your kingdom the first being last and the last first.
Help us, then, to trust in your purpose,
and to walk humbly with you.   *Nick Fawcett*

17   Lord Jesus Christ,
we look forward to that day when your kingdom shall come
and you are all in all.
Until then, we will trust in you,
secure in your love,
confident in your eternal purpose,
assured that your will shall be done.
To you be praise and glory, now and for evermore.

Nick Fawcett

18   Lord Jesus Christ,
we have come to worship you in this glad season of Advent,
a season of expectation,
of celebration,
and, above all, of preparation.
We come now, because we want to be ready –
ready to give thanks for your coming,
to recognise the ways you come to us now,
and to welcome you when you come again.
Open our hearts as we worship you,
so that all we share may give us a deeper understanding of
this season
and a fuller experience of your love.
In your name we ask it.

    Nick Fawcett

19   Lord Jesus Christ,
as you came once, so you shall come again
to establish your kingdom
and to fulfil the purpose of the One who sent you.
Help us to learn from your first coming
and to remember that,
despite the long years of expectation
and the desire of so many to see you,
few found room for you when you finally came.
Save us, then, from complacency,
and teach us to live each day to your glory,
happy at each moment to stand in your presence
and ready to welcome you on the day of your return.
In your name we pray.

    Nick Fawcett

20   Lord Jesus Christ,
prepare our hearts to meet you in this time of worship
and when you return in glory to establish your kingdom.
Confront, instruct and enable us by your Spirit,
so that we will be awake and alert,
equipped to live each moment
as though the day of your coming has dawned,
and ready to welcome you whenever it might be.

    Nick Fawcett

Second Sunday of Advent

21   Blessed are you, Lord our God,
for you are our Creator
and you have called us to know you
and proclaim your love.
Help us to be aware that you speak to us
through the Scriptures
and through those who tell
of your presence and power today.
Blessed are you, Father, Son and Holy Spirit.
God, we thank you for the prophets
who told us of your love and salvation.
We give thanks for Isaiah and Amos,
Jeremiah and Malachi,
Ezekiel and John the Baptist.
You are their God and our God:
you are their Father and our Father.
Help us to know that as you came to them
you come to us.   *David Adam*

22   Lord our God, we give you thanks
and rejoice in the great love that you have for us:
we rejoice in your presence and in your peace.
We pray for your whole Church
as it prepares for the Christmas season.
May it encourage people to come before you
in joy and in celebration.
Bless all who preach and all who teach the faith:
may they show the joy of knowing you and your love.
    David Adam

23   We pray that we and your whole Church
may be prepared for your coming to us.
When you come
may you find us a holy and a godly people;
may you find us striving for peace
and looking forward to your glory.   *David Adam*

Second week of Advent

24   Help us, Lord, in all our preparations for Christmas –
the writing of cards, buying of presents,
wrapping of gifts, decorating the home –
to make ready for you,
preparing ourselves in heart and mind to worship you afresh
and welcome you more fully into our lives,
so that when the day of your coming finally dawns,
we may be ready to greet you and celebrate a banquet,
not at our table,
but yours.   *Nick Fawcett*

25   Help us, Lord, to point to your way,
so that others in turn may find guidance in their journey
of life.
May all we say, do, think and are,
point away from us and towards you.   *Nick Fawcett*

26   Save us, Lord, from carelessness in our relationship with you,
from being casual and complacent in our dealings,
assuming we can gloss over whatever's wrong between us.
Teach us to work at our faith,
preparing the ground each day to know you better,
so that when your kingdom comes,
we may be ready to stand before you and meet you,
face to face.   *Nick Fawcett*

27   Lord Jesus Christ,
prepare our hearts to welcome you now,
and so may we be ready to welcome you
when you come again.   *Nick Fawcett*

28   Lord Jesus Christ,
teach us to anticipate your return
by preparing the way for your coming;
to catch a glimpse of your kingdom
through living by its values today.
Live in us now,
so that the day may come

when we live with you and all your people
for all eternity,
your will complete and your promise fulfilled.
In your name we ask it.   *Nick Fawcett*

29   Lord Jesus Christ,
we remember today that though your people longed for
your coming,
many were not prepared to welcome you,
failing to recognise you when you came.
Forgive us that we are equally closed sometimes
to your coming into our lives,
forcing you into a mould we have made for you,
presuming your thoughts and your ways are the same as ours.
Forgive us that our expectations are small and limited,
shaped by looking at life from a human rather than eternal
perspective.
Forgive us, and help us to be prepared.
Teach us to examine ourselves –
our words and deeds,
thoughts and attitudes –
and so to live each day open to what you would do in us
and through us,
to the glory of your name.   *Nick Fawcett*

30   Loving God,
we praise you that the light which dawned
in the life of Zechariah and Elizabeth,
that transformed the future for Mary and Joseph,
and that lit up the sky on the night of the Saviour's birth,
continues to shine today.
We thank you for the new beginning you have brought in
our lives,
and the light that continues to guide us.
Teach us to walk in that light day by day,
and so may each moment be a new dawn,
a new beginning,
rich in promise and filled by your love,
through Jesus Christ our Lord.   *Nick Fawcett*

31   Lord Jesus Christ,
you call us to test ourselves and to ensure that we are still in
the faith.
Help us to take that challenge seriously,
for we so easily imagine all is well when in fact much is wrong.
We talk of listening to your voice,
but hear what we want to hear.
We speak of seeking your will,
yet we prefer our way,
expecting you to conform to our expectations.
Draw close to us and fill us with your Spirit,
so that our faith may be as real and as fresh today
as the moment we first believed.
Prepare us for your coming again,
so that we may be ready to receive you
and found faithful in your service,
to the glory of your name.

Nick Fawcett

32   Lord Jesus Christ,
we thank you for all those who prepared the way for
your coming,
whether long ago in Bethlehem
or in countless hearts since that day.
We think especially of John the Baptist,
remembering his courage to speak the truth no matter what
the cost,
his readiness to point away from himself and towards
your light,
his willingness to live in such a way
that everything he did testified to the truth of his message
in a manner that words alone could never do.
Help us to prepare your way in turn,
witnessing to your renewing power
and demonstrating your compassion,
so that the hearts of many may be made ready to receive you
and to respond to your grace.
In your name we ask it.

Nick Fawcett

33   Lord Jesus Christ,
     we remember today the ministry of John the Baptist:
     his readiness to spend himself in your service,
     to proclaim the good news of your kingdom,
     to point away from himself
     and to seek your glory rather than his own.
     Forgive us that we find it so hard to follow his example,
     preferring instead the way of self-service,
     of putting our own interests before those of others.
     Help us to recognise that it is in giving we receive,
     and so may we commit our lives to you
     and bring glory to your name.   *Nick Fawcett*

34   Lord Jesus Christ,
     we come today yearning to welcome, worship, meet and
     greet you,
     but conscious also that,
     just as many were not ready to receive you
     when first you entered our world,
     so we too can be less prepared than we think,
     our narrow expectations or misplaced assumptions
     closing our minds to your presence among us. *Nick Fawcett*

35   Lord,
     we ask that, as we draw near to you,
     you will draw near to us,
     stirring our hearts and capturing our imagination.
     Prepare us to recognise you afresh at work in our lives and
     our world,
     and so make us ready to serve you, today and always.
                                                      Nick Fawcett

36   Lord,
     as you spoke through John the Baptist,
     and through the prophets before him,
     speak now through this time of worship,
     and through all who will share in leading it.
     Behind the voices we hear,
     the words we read and the message we listen to
     may we hear your voice,

calling, confronting,
leading, loving,
enthusing and enabling.
Open our ears, our minds and our souls
to your word of truth,
the Word made flesh,
Jesus Christ our Lord.   *Nick Fawcett*

37   Gracious God,
       help us, like John the Baptist before us
       and so many others who have followed in his footsteps,
       to see the light of Christ and bear witness to it,
       pointing through word and deed to his love for all.
       Open our lives, through your Spirit, to his presence among
       us now,
       and help us to live in such a way that his light may shine
       in us
       and through us,
       bringing glory to you.   *Nick Fawcett*

38   Father God,
       just as you sent your servant John into the wilderness
       to prepare the way of the Lord
       and to make ready your people to receive him,
       so prepare us now to respond afresh to the gift of Christ
       and to all that you offer us through him.
       Give us a readiness truly to listen, learn, worship and respond,
       receiving the forgiveness he extends
       and the renewal he makes possible,
       and giving back in return our heartfelt gratitude
       expressed in true commitment and faithful service.
       In his name we pray.   *Nick Fawcett*

39   Sovereign God,
       we are reminded today of how,
       through the prophets and the testimony of John the Baptist,
       you brought challenge as well as promise,
       a message that disturbed as much as it delighted,
       unsettled as well as uplifted.

Help us,
as we strive to follow Jesus,
to be open to your voice in the wilderness,
your word that probes deep within,
searching the thoughts of the heart
and confronting us with the challenge of the gospel.
However demanding it may be,
teach us to hear,
to listen
and to respond,
through Jesus Christ our Lord.   *Nick Fawcett*

Third Sunday of Advent

40   When we struggle to be faithful and to say our prayers,
      when we are willing to let go for the sake of God,
      when we attempt to proclaim the gospel,
      when we patiently await his coming,
      the Lord comes as he came to John the Baptist.
                                                   David Adam

41   As we remember John the Baptist and all the prophets,
      we give thanks for men and women of vision
      through the ages.
      We ask you to guide and bless
      all preachers of the word and ministers of the sacraments,
      all who teach the faith
      and all who influence our daily lives.
      We pray for all who are struggling
      for freedom in their faith
      and for those who are imprisoned because of their beliefs.
                                                   David Adam

42   Blessed are you, Lord our God,
      for you sent the prophets and John the Baptist
      to prepare your way.
      You have told us of your coming
      and you reveal yourself to us in Jesus.
      You come to each of us in power and in love.   *David Adam*

43   Blessed are you, Lord our God,
for you send your messengers and prophets
to tell of your coming.
As John the Baptist was a burning and shining light
in the darkness,
help us to show your presence in our daily life. *David Adam*

44   God, we thank you for Zechariah and Elizabeth
and for the birth of their son, John the Baptist.
We give thanks that he prepared the way
for the coming of Jesus.
Grant that we who are baptised may be ready
for the coming of our Lord.
You are their God and our God:
you are their Father and our Father.
Help us to know that as you came to them
you come to us.   *David Adam*

45   Blessed are you, Lord God of all creation,
to you be praise and glory for ever!
Your messenger, John the Baptist,
was a shining and burning light in the darkness.
He spoke the words of a prophet
and proclaimed forgiveness and the kingdom.
He prepared the way for the coming of the Lord.
May we share in his witness to the light
that true Light come into the world,
and rejoice that the Christ dispels our darkness.
       David Adam

46   Inspire us, O Lord, by the life and teaching of John
the Baptist.
May we learn to live simply, that others may simply live:
let us turn to you each day and rise in your presence.
Let us seek forgiveness of all that is past and direction for
the future,
that we may be heralds of Christ and prepare for his
coming;
that we may live and work for his kingdom, where you reign.
       David Adam

47 Lord, inspire us by the life of John the Baptist
    that we may live simply
    so that others may simply live.
    Let us turn to you and your love each day
    and seek forgiveness of our sins,
    so that we may walk in newness of life.   *David Adam*

Third week of Advent

48 Remind us, Lord, that you alone truly know the future,
    your promises of old having found fulfilment in Christ,
    the message of the law and prophets vindicated by his birth,
    death and resurrection.
    Help us, remembering all you have so faithfully done,
    to trust in all you will yet do,
    confident that, in the fullness of time,
    your will shall be done and your kingdom come.
                                                   Nick Fawcett

49 When we look at the world, Lord –
    its tensions and suffering, need and heartbreak –
    it's hard not to wonder what you're doing
    and why you take so long to put things right,
    for much there seems to question your love
    and undermine your will.
    Help us to understand, though,
    that there are no quick fixes to such things,
    no short-term solutions,
    but that you are working nonetheless,
    your purpose destined to triumph,
    not in our time, but in yours.   *Nick Fawcett*

50 Loving God,
    teach us that your gracious purpose
    goes back to the beginning of time,
    and that it will endure until the end of time,
    and beyond.   *Nick Fawcett*

51   Gracious God,
your word was active from the beginning.
It brought life itself into existence,
and controls the destiny of everything you have created.
What you have decreed shall be,
for no word of yours returns to you empty.
Help us, then, to listen to what you would say to us
both today and throughout this season of Advent.
Open our ears, our hearts and our minds,
so that we may hear your voice and respond in joyful service,
through Jesus Christ our Lord.   *Nick Fawcett*

52   Living God,
you spoke,
and the world was brought into being –
the heavens and the earth,
the sea and dry land,
night and day,
life in all its variety and abundance.
You spoke again in the book of the Law,
the poetry of the psalms,
the wisdom of the teacher,
the chronicling of history
and the message of the prophets,
revealing your will,
proclaiming your purpose.
You spoke through Jesus Christ, the Word made flesh,
through those who witnessed to his life and ministry,
and through those who across the years have shared
in the building of his Church.
You have spoken throughout history:
through preaching and teaching,
through study and quiet devotion,
through prayer and fellowship,
through the wonder of this world;
and still you speak today,
your word ever old but always new,
able to redeem,
renew and restore.

Speak to us now, we pray.
Help us to use this season of Advent
to listen more carefully to your voice,
and so to walk with you more closely,
this and every day,
through Jesus Christ our Lord. *Nick Fawcett*

53   Loving God,
from earliest times you have been at work in our world,
striving to fulfil your purposes,
preparing the way for the coming of your kingdom.
We praise you for the witness of the prophets
foretelling the coming of the Messiah.
We praise you for the ministry of John the Baptist,
a voice in the wilderness calling people to repentance,
making ready the way of the Lord.
We praise you for those who made the gospel known to us,
giving us the opportunity to respond.
Help us now truly to prepare for Christmas,
not simply outwardly but inwardly,
so that we may joyfully celebrate the birth of Christ
and receive him into our lives.
In his name we ask it. *Nick Fawcett*

54   Eternal God,
we celebrate today the fulfilment of your promises of old
through the coming of the Messiah,
foretold by the prophets and long yearned for –
a Saviour to deliver your people and establish your
kingdom,
bringing freedom, life and new beginnings.
We celebrate how wonderfully you honoured those
promises in Christ,
granting through him more than we can ever ask or imagine.
Help us now, as we worship you, to celebrate your faithfulness
and to trust you completely for the future,
knowing that we can depend on you, come what may,
certain that what you have pledged will be accomplished
and that nothing can ever separate us from your love
in Jesus Christ our Lord. *Nick Fawcett*

55   Gracious God,
we come to reflect again on your age-old promises,
on your sovereign purpose,
on your constant working within human history.
We remember that you brought this world into being,
that you guided your people across the centuries,
despite repeated rebellion and disobedience,
and that, through your great love,
you took on human flesh,
coming to our world through Jesus Christ.
We rejoice in all he showed of you
through his birth in Bethlehem,
his life and ministry,
his death and resurrection,
and we celebrate his living presence with us now through
his Spirit.
Open our hearts to everything you would say to us through
this day,
so that we may understand your love more completely
and serve you more faithfully,
in his name.   *Nick Fawcett*

56   Sovereign God,
we thank you for all who have borne witness to your
coming in Christ,
all who have shared their faith
so that others might come to know him
and experience his love for themselves.
We thank you for those from whom we first heard the gospel,
and all who have nurtured and encouraged us in discipleship.
Help us now to play our part in that continuing ministry,
sharing what Christ means to those around us,
and making known the way he has worked in our lives.
Send us out in his name, to his glory.   *Nick Fawcett*

57   Loving God,
we celebrate today the fulfilment of your word across
the years.
You promised Abraham that through his offspring
all the earth would be blessed –

and it was.
You promised through your prophets that the Messiah
would come –
and he came.
You promised Mary that she would give birth to a son –
and she did.
You promised the disciples that death would not be the end –
and it wasn't.
You promised your followers that they would receive the
Holy Spirit –
and it happened.
Teach us, then, to trust you for the present and the future,
knowing that you are always faithful,
and that you will accomplish whatever you have pledged
to do.
Teach us to be faithful to you in all our dealings,
just as you are invariably faithful to us.
In Christ's name we ask it.   *Nick Fawcett*

58   Loving God, we praise you
      for fulfilling your age-long purpose
      through the birth of Jesus.
      We thank you that your promises are not simply empty words
      like so many of ours,
      but pledges we can rely on,
      knowing they will always be honoured.
      Teach us, then, to read the Scriptures
      hearing your word revealed in Christ
      and trusting in the promise of new life
      you have given us through him.   *Nick Fawcett*

59   Loving God,
      for all our faith
      there are some things we consider beyond us
      and beyond you.
      Belief says one thing but realism another,
      and in consequence we set limits
      to the way you are able to work in our lives.
      Yet time and again you have overturned human
      expectations,

demonstrating that all things are possible
for those who love you.
Teach us, then,
to look beyond the obvious and immediate,
and to live rather in the light of your sovereign grace
which is able to do far more
than we can ever ask or imagine;
through Jesus Christ our Lord. *Nick Fawcett*

60 Gracious God,
we thank you for the gift of words
through which we are able to express so much.
We thank you for the words of Scripture
that speak so powerfully of your love.
But most of all we thank you
for putting your words into action,
making them come alive in the person of Jesus.
Help us in our turn not simply to use words
but to act upon them,
not just to talk about faith
but to live it day by day. *Nick Fawcett*

Fourth Sunday of Advent

61 Blessed are you, Lord God of all creation.
To you be praise and glory for ever!
In the darkness of this passing age your light has shone out.
You have not forced yourself upon us,
but you only come if we so will it.
As we rejoice in the obedience of Mary, the blessed Virgin,
may we accept you into our lives and homes,
knowing that you have come to dwell among us.

David Adam

62 Lord God, we give you thanks for Joseph
and for his courage to do your will.
Help us to bring in your kingdom
by our obedience to you this day and always.
May we show that we dwell in you and you in us.

David Adam

63   God, we thank you for the obedience of Mary
       and for all who help to bring in your kingdom
       by seeking to do your will.
       We give thanks
       for your faithful people throughout all ages.
       Lord, guide your Church
       that it may know your will and serve you faithfully.

David Adam

64   God, we thank you
       for the message of the angel Gabriel to Mary.
       May we learn the obedience of Mary,
       serving you with joy and accepting Jesus into our lives.
       You are her God and our God:
       you are her Father and our Father.
       Help us to know that as you came to Mary
       you come to us.   *David Adam*

65   Come, Lord, be known among us.
       As you came to earth, born of Mary,
       come into our hearts and homes.
       As you became a little child,
       help us to grow in awareness of you.
       As you walked this earth,
       help us to walk and work with you.
       May the bright light of Christ enlighten our hearts,
       shine in our minds, direct our journeying,
       and scatter the darkness from the world.   *David Adam*

66   God, as we prepare for Christmas
       may we be ready for your coming to us.
       As we make space for friends and relatives
       may we make room for you to be born within us
       as you were born within Mary.
       In our daily living let us seek to do your will
       and help to bring in your kingdom.   *David Adam*

Fourth week of Advent

67 Forgive us, Lord,
  for so often we're disobedient,
  ignoring your call and defying your will,
  preferring our way to yours.
  Teach us, instead, like Mary long ago,
  to listen to your voice and humbly to obey,
  putting your will before our own –
  self second and you first. *Nick Fawcett*

68 Redeemer God,
  as we prepare to celebrate the birth of your Son,
  speak through the singing of hymns,
  the reading of Scripture,
  the preaching of your word,
  the offering of prayers –
  these and so much more.
  Break through all that separates us from you and him:
  over-familiarity,
  indifference,
  self-will,
  disobedience,
  narrowness of vision,
  weakness of resolve.
  Move among us through your Spirit –
  inspiring,
  instructing,
  revealing,
  renewing –
  so that we may be equipped to worship
  and serve you. *Nick Fawcett*

69 Almighty God,
  we recall at this joyful season how,
  through her willingness to hear your word
  and commit herself to your service,
  you were able to use Mary to fulfil your purpose,
  entering our world,

inaugurating your kingdom
and bringing closer that day when sorrow and suffering,
darkness and death will be no more.
Help us, then, as we gather now to worship,
to hear your word
and to respond with similar obedience,
prepared to be used as you see fit.
Through our discipleship,
weak and feeble though it might be,
may your grace be revealed,
your love made known
and your world enriched.   *Nick Fawcett*

70   Lord Jesus Christ,
       born to Mary,
       coming to our world through her,
       be born afresh in us
       that we might be born again through you.
       Touch now this time of worship
       that the message of your birth,
       so familiar and well loved,
       will speak afresh with new power and clarity,
       thrilling our hearts
       and filling us with joy and gratitude.
       Draw close to us now,
       that through welcoming you into our lives
       and opening ourselves once more to your renewing power
       you may reach out through us to the world,
       bringing hope and healing, light and life,
       to the glory of your name.   *Nick Fawcett*

71   Lord Jesus Christ,
       you promise that when two or three are gathered in
       your name,
       you will be there among them.
       Help us to trust in that promise –
       to know you are here
       and to meet with you now through the inner presence of
       your Holy Spirit.

Open our eyes to your presence,
speak again your word of life,
and help us to listen,
to believe
and to respond,
to the glory of your name.   *Nick Fawcett*

72   Lord Jesus Christ,
      we know and love the message of Christmas so well,
      perhaps too well –
      for we have heard and celebrated it so many times
      and can assume we have understood all it has to say to us.
      Save us from that danger,
      and help us to reflect on what your coming means
      for us,
      for others,
      for all;
      for yesterday,
      today
      and tomorrow.
      Speak to us now,
      through readings,
      through music,
      through prayer,
      through your Spirit at work within us.
      Speak through all we shall share together,
      nurturing our faith,
      strengthening our commitment
      and expanding our love for you and for all.
      In your name we ask it.   *Nick Fawcett*

73   Almighty God,
      you are greater than our minds can fathom,
      higher than our highest thoughts,
      sovereign over all,
      worthy of praise and honour.
      Forgive us that we sometimes lose
      our sense of awe and wonder in your presence,
      oblivious to your greatness and forgetful of your goodness.

Speak to us,
as you spoke to Mary,
and help us to catch a new sense of who you are,
of all you have done,
and of all you will yet do in our lives.
Help us to magnify your name,
singing your praises and telling of your greatness,
through Jesus Christ our Lord.   *Nick Fawcett*

74   Gracious God,
you came to our world in fulfilment of your promises of old,
your word embodied in a child lying in a manger.
You loved us so much that you staked everything
to break down the barriers that keep us from you.
You shared our humanity from birth to death,
so that with you we might share your eternity,
life in all its fullness.
You became God with us,
so that we might become one with you.
Teach us that, as you needed Mary's response then,
you long for our response now:
our willingness to accept your mercy
and to experience the blessings you so long to give us.
Come again now and be born in our hearts,
so that we may truly love you and joyfully serve you,
this and every day,
through Jesus Christ our Lord.   *Nick Fawcett*

75   Gracious God,
we praise you for this season of Advent,
this time for rejoicing and celebration,
praise and worship,
exulting in your goodness.
We praise you for coming in Christ,
bringing in a new kingdom
and anticipating an era of peace and justice
when the poor will have plenty,
the hungry be fed,
and the lowly be lifted up.

We praise you that you want us to be a part of that,
not just to share in it but also to play a part in bringing it
to pass.
Forgive us that we sometimes lose sight of your purpose
and underestimate your greatness.
Open our eyes to the breadth of your love,
the wonder of your mercy and the extent of your goodness,
and so may we give you the worship and adoration that is
due to you,
this and every day,
through Jesus Christ our Lord.   *Nick Fawcett*

76   Loving God,
the great festival of Christmas is drawing nearer
and we are busy preparing for it –
choosing presents,
writing cards,
planning get-togethers,
buying food –
so much that has become an accepted and expected part of
this season.
Yet, in all the bustle, we so easily forget what matters most:
responding to the gift of your Son.
Forgive us for relegating Jesus to the periphery of our
celebrations
rather than placing him at the centre where he belongs;
for doing so much to prepare for Christmas on the surface
yet so little to make ourselves ready within.
Open our hearts to welcome the living Christ into our lives,
and so may we rejoice in his love,
not just at Christmas, but always.
In his name we ask it.   *Nick Fawcett*

77   Gracious God,
reminded at this season of your awesome gift in Christ,
we want to respond,
to offer something in return as a sign of our gratitude
for all you have done and continue to do.
We would bring you our worship –
not just well-intentioned thoughts and words

209 We pray that the light of the world
     may shine so brightly in our lives
     that other people notice it
     and are attracted to you
     by the way we live and love.   *Susan Sayers*

210 We thank you that through your love
     we can receive so many joys and blessings in our lives.
     We thank you especially for the relationships
     which enrich our lives so much.   *Susan Sayers*

211 Sometimes, Lord, Christmas can be a sad and lonely season,
     bringing to the surface memories, anxieties or dangers.
     Keep our hearts and minds in the knowledge
     that you are with us always,
     through both good and difficult times.   *Susan Sayers*

212 Lord Jesus,
     may we truly be the Body of Christ,
     in loving servanthood, humility and availability;
     that as pastors and teachers,
     prophets and evangelists,
     givers, carers and listeners,
     we, the people of God, may make Christ known.

                                                Susan Sayers

213 Father God,
     may your Word of life
     encourage us on our journey
     and bring us safely to your eternal kingdom.   *Susan Sayers*

214 Emmanuel, God with us:
     we welcome you!
     As we celebrate God's coming to us
     as a human child,
     we bring the needs of our world
     before you, the God we can trust.   *Susan Sayers*

203   Lord our God,
      we thank you for Christmas joy
      and all the opportunities
      to show our love for one another.
      May our love, rooted in yours,
      continue throughout the year.   *Susan Sayers*

204   As the world is reminded
      of love and peace
      in the words of the carols,
      may the reality of a God
      who loves us so much
      transform our social
      and political thinking,
      and energise our plans
      and negotiations.   *Susan Sayers*

205   As we celebrate Christmas,
      when the Word of God became flesh,
      may we so be filled with God's loving life
      that our actions touch the world
      with hope which lasts
      even when Christmas decorations are put away. *Susan Sayers*

206   As Christmas brings together
      family members and friends,
      and we make contact with those we seldom meet,
      may all our relationships be nourished
      with love and forgiveness,
      and may we value one another more.   *Susan Sayers*

207   Father, we can never thank you enough
      for coming to rescue us,
      and we praise you now and in our lives.   *Susan Sayers*

208   This Christmas we pray that we may stop
      our noise, chatter and arguing long enough
      to hear the angels singing of hope and peace.   *Susan Sayers*

197   Lord God, thank you for healing me
with the blessing of your forgiveness.
Thank you for your generous, shining love
that changes crusted lives and broken spirits.
Thank you that you love us as we are
and are happy to enlist our help
in the lighting of dark places,
bringing hope and joy.
Blessed be God for ever.   *Susan Sayers*

198   A grace to say at your Christmas dinner:
Lord Jesus, born in Bethlehem
on the first Christmas Day,
welcome to this meal with us.
We give thanks to God for food on the table
and for the love and fellowship we share.
As we eat and drink to celebrate Christmas,
may we know your love in our hearts.   *Susan Sayers*

199   Father, as we celebrate the birth of Jesus, your Word,
we thank you with our whole heart.
The bells and lights and presents and decorations
in church and in our homes
express our thanks to you, Lord,
for coming into the world in person.   *Susan Sayers*

200   Thank you for being prepared
to face the dangers and risks
of human mistakes and sin
in order to save us.   *Susan Sayers*

201   For all the many blessings of this past year
and for all the good that you have enabled us to do;
for the experiences that have taught us
humility and patience,
we thank you.   *Susan Sayers*

202   Lord God, we thank you for our world
and all its beauty and blessing.
Teach us your ways, your love and your truth,
and let your kingdom grow and flourish.   *Susan Sayers*

Enable us, then, to live each day with joy in our hearts
and wonder in our eyes
as we share the love you have shown us
and make known the great thing you have done in Christ.
In his name we ask it.   *Nick Fawcett*

192 The world Jesus was born into
     was the world we know.
     Thank you for being prepared
     to face the dangers and risks
     of human mistakes and sin
     in order to save us.   *Susan Sayers*

193 Many of us will be celebrating
     with our families and friends.
     We invite you to join us in all the festivities,
     and ask you to teach us true loving.   *Susan Sayers*

194 As we celebrate Christmas,
     when the Word of God became flesh,
     we pray for the Church, the Body of Christ.
     May we be so filled with God's loving life
     that our actions touch the world with hope
     which lasts even when Christmas decorations
     are put away.   *Susan Sayers*

195 Thank you, Jesus,
     for being born
     into our world.
     Thank you for showing us
     God's love.   *Susan Sayers*

196 Here I offer you, Lord Jesus,
     all my preparations for Christmas.
     Teach me more about giving
     and more about receiving.
     Realign my priorities
     in tune with your will,
     and enable me to see more clearly
     how best to celebrate your coming
     as our Lord and Saviour.   *Susan Sayers*

yet delivers little,
help us today and always
to celebrate your Word made flesh,
love incarnate –
a gift beyond price that will never disappoint.   *Nick Fawcett*

189 For so many, Lord,
Christmas stirs a sense of your presence,
reminding them of a reality beyond this world,
a relationship they crave,
yet all too quickly they forget,
so few finding you for themselves.
Break through the trappings of this season,
and touch human hearts the world over,
so that instead of being briefly remembered,
you may be known and loved,
this and every day.   *Nick Fawcett*

190 At this time of family get-togethers, Lord,
open our eyes to the wider family of the Church
and of all people across the world.
May Christmas truly be a time of coming together;
a time when,
remembering the One made flesh,
we grow together,
united in your love,
and celebrating our common humanity,
barriers broken and divisions overcome.   *Nick Fawcett*

191 Living God,
we remember today
how shepherds responded to the message of the angels –
how they hurried to Bethlehem
and found the baby lying in a manger,
and how afterwards they went on their way,
sharing what they had seen and heard.
Teach us to share our experience of Christ in turn.
Help us to understand that your coming through him
is good news for everyone,
and that you want us to help make that known.

186   Loving God,
      as the years go by and life drifts on,
      sometimes we too, like Anna,
      find it hard to keep faith alive.
      As we face life's repeated disappointments,
      as prayer after prayer seems to go unanswered,
      so faith falters,
      the dreams of youth dulled by the reality of experience.
      Yet you tell us through Jesus
      never to stop looking forward,
      never to stop believing in the future.
      Lord Jesus Christ, help us to go on
      trusting in the victory of your love
      and the coming of your kingdom
      despite everything that seems to deny it.   *Nick Fawcett*

187   Forgive us, Lord,
      for we fritter away money on trivialities
      while a world goes hungry,
      this season of goodwill to all
      turned into one of good things for us.
      Teach us to make room in our celebrations
      for those who,
      in this life,
      have so little to celebrate,
      and to give as generously to them
      as you have given to us.   *Nick Fawcett*

188   For so many, Lord,
      despite the glitz, bustle,
      hype and expense,
      it's not just crackers but Christmas itself
      that proves to be a let-down,
      promising much yet delivering little.
      Awaken the hearts of all to the glorious surprise
      at the heart of this season –
      the wonder of your Son,
      born in a stable and laid in a manger.
      Instead of focusing on trivia that promises much

Help us to receive it with both our minds and our hearts,
always looking to understand more of what it continues
to say.
And help us to share what Christ has done for us
so that others in turn may celebrate
what he has done for them.   *Nick Fawcett*

184   Lord Jesus Christ,
we remember today that those who first heard the good news
were not the religious elite or those respected in the eyes of
the world,
but shepherds –
ordinary, everyday people like each of us.
We remember how, throughout your ministry,
you welcomed those whom society had little time for,
who were counted as nothing;
those who would have known their need
and made no presumption on your goodness.
Teach us, through their experience,
that, whoever we are,
however insignificant we may feel,
you value us for who we are,
accept us despite our faults,
and love us come what may.
May that knowledge be good news for us
this and every day.   *Nick Fawcett*

185   Loving God,
challenge us through the example of the shepherds.
Teach us that it is not enough to accept the claims of
the gospel
on the basis of what someone else has said,
but that we need to experience the truth of it for ourselves.
Help us, then, to open our souls to the presence of Christ,
and to welcome him into our lives.
Help us to know the reality of his Spirit at work within us,
and to accept the message of the gospel,
not just with our heads but also with our hearts.
In the name of Christ, we ask it.   *Nick Fawcett*

'I am the Lord's servant.
Let it be to me just as you say.'
In Jesus' name we pray.   *Nick Fawcett*

181 Loving God,
     remind us that in taking flesh and being born as a baby,
     you identified yourself fully with humankind,
     not imposing yourself upon us
     but drawing alongside,
     inviting a response.
     Remind us that you made yourself vulnerable,
     exposing yourself to persecution and rejection from
     the beginning,
     willingly bearing the price of love.
     Open our hearts today to respond –
     freely, gladly and reverently –
     ready to risk something for you
     who risked so much for us.   *Nick Fawcett*

182 God of love,
     recalling today how shepherds hurried to Bethlehem,
     eager to see for themselves the truth of what they had heard,
     so we too are hungry to meet afresh with Christ,
     to offer him our worship,
     to rejoice in his presence
     and to make our personal response to your coming
     through him.
     Direct, then, our thoughts and actions in this time
     of worship,
     so that through our hymns, readings, prayers,
     reflection and fellowship
     we may see and know you better,
     appreciating more fully the wonder of this season
     and the good news it proclaims for all.   *Nick Fawcett*

183 Loving God,
     you have given us and all the world
     good news in Christ.
     Help us to hear it afresh each day,
     recognising it as news for us.

177 Living God,
    teach us that the joyful message
    proclaimed at Bethlehem all those years ago
    is good news for us today,
    here and now.   *Nick Fawcett*

178 Lord Jesus,
    child in the manger,
    man on the cross,
    risen Saviour,
    Lord of all,
    be born in us today.   *Nick Fawcett*

179 Gracious God,
    help us to learn from the example of Mary.
    Teach us this Christmas time
    to ponder, as she did, all that you have said and done:
    to listen again to familiar readings and carols,
    and to hear again the story we know so well,
    but also to consider what it all might mean;
    what you are saying not just to others but also to us.
    Amid all the celebrations and rejoicing,
    help us to be still before you
    so that we may open our hearts to your living word,
    your renewing love
    and your redeeming power,
    and so know the presence of Jesus within us,
    by his grace.   *Nick Fawcett*

180 Gracious God,
    you may not ask of us what you asked of Mary,
    but your challenge comes nonetheless
    calling us to avenues of service that we would never
    imagine possible.
    Whoever we are,
    we all have a part to play in your purpose.
    Grant us the humility we need to hear your voice
    and the faith we need to respond.
    Like Mary,
    let each of us be ready to answer when you call:

173 Teach us, Lord,
that your coming into the world was not without cost;
that you gave of yourself,
surrendering your life to bring us light.
Help us, as we celebrate your birth,
to remember also your death,
and to be ready in turn to give
as well as receive
in the service of your kingdom.   *Nick Fawcett*

174 Teach us, Lord,
amid the festivity and merriment of this season,
to delve deeper,
discovering what's of real value within it:
the new life you offer through your Son,
bringing nourishment to body, mind and soul.
Help us to find for ourselves
that most precious gift of all.   *Nick Fawcett*

175 Open our hearts, Lord,
to the radiance of your love,
the light that shone in the birth of your Son
and that continues to shine today,
nothing able to overcome it.
Help us to glimpse afresh the true romance of this season,
the full wonder and beauty of it all,
able to shed light in our hearts
not just at Christmas
but each moment of every day.   *Nick Fawcett*

176 Loving God,
grant that the faith we profess in Christ
may be as real tomorrow and every day as it is now.
Grant that, when Christmas is over,
the good news at its heart will continue to shape our lives
and that we will continue to offer the one at its centre
our wholehearted discipleship.
In his name we pray.   *Nick Fawcett*

We thank you that, whatever we face, you are with us
through him,
supporting us by your love,
enriching us by your grace,
equipping us through your Spirit.
Inspire us afresh each day with the good news of Christ
and the reality of his presence in our hearts,
so that we may go on our way rejoicing,
now and always.   *Nick Fawcett*

170   Remind us, Lord,
      that after the stable came a cross,
      after birth, death,
      after celebration, sacrifice,
      and after pleasure, pain,
      each bound by a single stem:
      the wonder of your love.
      Help us to rejoice in all that this season means,
      not just in part,
      but in full.   *Nick Fawcett*

171   Teach us, Lord,
      to put you at the centre of Christmas,
      so that it may transform our lives –
      the things we do,
      the way we think,
      the people we are,
      the church we long to be –
      each touched by your presence
      and made new by your love.   *Nick Fawcett*

172   Loving Lord,
      keep alive in us the hopefulness of youth,
      that same sense of joy in simple things
      and expectation for the future.
      Though life dishes out knocks and disappointments,
      help us to carry on believing
      in what you hold in store –
      wonderful beyond words.   *Nick Fawcett*

167   Thank you, Lord,
for your love,
constantly reaching out
though we fail to appreciate all you've given
or how much it cost you.
Thank you that your blessing and goodness
is not dependent on our deserving,
but goes on being poured out day after day,
generous beyond measure.   *Nick Fawcett*

168   Gracious God,
we thank you for the glorious message of this season:
the glad tidings of great joy,
ever old yet ever new.
We thank you for the faith of Mary,
the commitment of Joseph,
the message of the angels
and the response of the shepherds –
the way you changed their lives that day in Bethlehem.
Above all, though,
we thank you that you have changed our lives too;
that the good news these heard and responded to long ago
is news still today –
as special now as then,
and for us as much as anyone!
Teach us never to forget that wonderful truth;
never to overlook the fact that you have come to us in Christ.
May that knowledge burn brightly in our hearts,
a constant source of joy and inspiration,
whatever life may bring.
In the name of Christ, we ask it.   *Nick Fawcett*

169   Gracious God,
we thank you for the joy of Christmas time:
the joy you gave to Mary, shepherds and magi
as you entered the world in Christ;
the joy you have brought to generations across the centuries
as they have come to faith;
the joy you offer us now
in a living and saving knowledge of Jesus Christ.

164   Lord Jesus Christ,
      we recall that you came to our world,
      to your people,
      yet among so many found no welcome.
      From the very beginning the majority shut you out,
      and of those who did accept you
      many did so only half-heartedly.
      Forgive us that sometimes we do the same.
      Help us to make room for you,
      and to give you not just a token place,
      but one at the very centre of our lives.   *Nick Fawcett*

165   Thank you, Lord,
      for the closeness you make possible with you,
      the relationship you have opened up
      through your coming among us,
      sharing our humanity
      and dying our death to bring us life.
      Help us to celebrate the love at the heart of this season –
      your gift of Christ –
      and, through him,
      draw us closer to you each day.   *Nick Fawcett*

166   Though much of the packaging surrounding Christmas
      needs discarding, Lord,
      save us from overlooking the love and care
      you showed in preparing the way of Christ.
      Help us,
      if we would fully celebrate your gift,
      to appreciate the context in which you gave it –
      the history of your people,
      teaching of the Law,
      and message of the prophets,
      each finding glorious fulfilment in the Word made flesh.
      For your Son,
      and all that points to him and your love,
      thank you!   *Nick Fawcett*

162 Loving God,
 remind us again that you are a God of grace,
 reaching out to the bad as well as the good,
 to sinners as well as saints.
 Teach us that you chose Mary,
 representative of the powerless;
 shepherds,
 examples of the socially marginalised;
 and countless others across the years whom society had
 rejected.
 Help us, then, to turn to you,
 acknowledging our faults and weaknesses,
 knowing that, despite them all,
 you have a place for us in your kingdom,
 through Jesus Christ our Lord.   *Nick Fawcett*

163 Loving God,
 we thank you for the great truth at the heart of this season –
 your coming to our world in Christ.
 We praise you that you go on coming,
 day after day,
 not just to others but also to us,
 meeting and working within us through your Holy Spirit.
 Forgive us everything that obstructs your coming –
 all the trivia and irrelevancies with which we fill our lives
 at the cost of time for you;
 all the cares, doubts and unbelief
 that prevent us sometimes from even glimpsing your presence.
 Come afresh now,
 and break through all the barriers in our lives,
 so that we may know you more nearly by our side
 and draw yet closer to you than we have ever been before.
 Speak your word,
 grant your guidance,
 confer your power
 and fill us with your love,
 so that we may serve you as faithfully
 as you have served us in Christ.
 In his name we ask it.   *Nick Fawcett*

We thank you for the way that message has spoken to us,
shown to be glad tidings in so many ways.
Yet we confess that we sometimes lose our initial sense of awe
and wonder,
and no longer feel the urge to respond to your love
as powerfully as we once did.
Forgive us for becoming casual and complacent in our faith,
failing to make time to worship,
and forgetting the need to nurture our relationship with you.
Speak to us again,
meet us through the living Christ,
and open our hearts to the renewing touch of your
Holy Spirit.
So may we catch again the sense of urgency felt by
the shepherds
as they rushed to Bethlehem,
and may the wonder of your love burn within us each day,
to your glory.   *Nick Fawcett*

161   Lord Jesus Christ,
we remember today how you came to our world
and found no welcome;
how, from the very beginning,
you were shut out,
no room for you even in the inn.
Forgive us that we are sometimes guilty of shutting you out
in turn,
failing to make room for you in so many areas of our lives.
Despite our words of faith and commitment,
we turn our back on you
when we would rather not face your challenge.
Forgive us,
and help us to make room for you,
not just this Christmas but always.
Teach us to give you not merely a token place in our hearts,
but to put you at the very centre of our lives.
Come now,
and make your home within us,
by your grace.   *Nick Fawcett*

or relegate you to the margins,
include you almost as an afterthought?
Forgive us, for all too often,
at Christmas or otherwise,
we have time for just about everything . . .
except you.   *Nick Fawcett*

158   Forgive us, Lord,
for we fail to reflect on our lives,
to weigh them in the balance,
ensuring we've got things right.
We become casual,
complacent,
accepting the status quo with barely a second thought.
Whatever else we do this season,
teach us to make room for the things that really matter;
room,
above all,
for you.   *Nick Fawcett*

159   Forgive us, Lord,
for we know this season so well,
its message so familiar,
that it no longer moves us,
no longer speaks as it once did.
Help us to see beyond the festive trappings and traditions
to the awesome truth they proclaim:
your Word, your Son,
your love, your gift –
good news,
now and always.   *Nick Fawcett*

160   Gracious God,
we thank you that you have given us good news in Christ,
a message that has thrilled generations across the years,
uplifting,
encouraging,
challenging
and renewing.

sovereign over all,
worthy of praise and honour.
Forgive us that all too often
we have lost our sense of awe and wonder before you.
Speak to us, as you spoke to Mary,
and help us to catch a new sense
of who you are and what you have done through Jesus.
Help us to magnify your name,
singing your praises
and telling of your greatness.   *Nick Fawcett*

156 Lord Jesus Christ,
you were born so that you might die.
You took on our humanity
so that you might experience also our mortality.
Only through identifying yourself so totally with us
could you bridge the gap that separates us from God.
You showed us the way of love,
and you followed it through to the end.
You proclaimed forgiveness,
and you paid the price to make it possible.
In life and in death, you testified to the grace of the Father,
and his purpose for all the world.
Help us, as we celebrate again your birth,
never to forget that this was just the beginning of the story.
As we greet you now as the child of Bethlehem,
so let us greet you also as the crucified Saviour
and the risen Lord,
and may we offer you,
this and every day,
our joyful worship
in grateful praise.   *Nick Fawcett*

157 How much time, Lord,
will we make for you this Christmas?
How much time,
before, during and after the celebrations,
to reflect on your love?
Will we put you at the centre of our celebrations,
the heart of our lives,

May we, like them, thrill to the good news of your coming,
and go on our way rejoicing,
making known to those we meet
everything we have found to be true in you.
In your name we pray.   *Nick Fawcett*

153   Lord Jesus Christ,
we celebrate today how wise men were prepared to seek,
and keep on seeking,
persevering despite setbacks and disappointments
until they found you.
We remember how you promised that all who seek will find,
that those who ask will receive,
that to those who knock the door will be opened,
and so we come now,
asking for your guidance and seeking to know you better,
so that, drawing ever closer to you,
we may offer our love and our lives in glad response,
to the glory of your name.   *Nick Fawcett*

154   Living God,
like Anna and Simeon before us,
may our hearts leap for joy as we celebrate your coming
in Christ,
the one anticipated for so long
and on whom the hopes of so many rested.
Help us to recognise in him the fulfilment of your promises
and answer to our needs;
the one who brings unsettling challenge yet also offers peace;
who brings light and life
not only to us but also to all the world.
Teach us to respond faithfully,
offering our grateful praise,
and witnessing in word and deed
to everything you have done through him.
In his name we pray.   *Nick Fawcett*

155   Almighty God,
you are greater than our minds can fathom,
higher than our highest thoughts,

offering you our heartfelt worship and joyful praise
for your gift beyond words,
Jesus Christ our Lord.   *Nick Fawcett*

150   Sovereign God,
       though we have heard it so many times before,
       and though the words of readings and carols we will
       share today
       are so familiar we know them almost back to front,
       grant that through the worship we bring you
       our hearts may thrill again to the good news of Christ,
       and our spirits soar at the message of his coming.
       Grant us new insights and deeper understanding,
       so that our faith may be enriched and our joy increased
       as we celebrate the great gift of your Son –
       glad tidings yesterday,
       today
       and every day.   *Nick Fawcett*

151   Lord Jesus Christ,
       come among us in this time of worship.
       As you came in Bethlehem and will come again in glory,
       so, we ask, draw near now
       and open our eyes to your presence among us here.
       Speak your word,
       impart your blessing,
       grant your mercy
       and renew our faith,
       so that we may be ready at every moment to welcome you
       and be equipped to live more truly to your praise and glory.
                                                         Nick Fawcett

152   Lord Jesus Christ,
       like the shepherds of old
       we come with hearts ablaze to celebrate your birth,
       to kneel in wonder,
       to offer our thanksgiving
       and to respond personally to you.

they went on their way rejoicing.
We remember how Simeon held you in his arms,
and with praise in his heart gave thanks to you.
We remember how generations since
have seen your face revealed in Christ,
and through him heard you speaking in a new way.
We remember the past
so that we might discover you in the present
and find faith for the future.
Be born in our hearts today
that we may be born again to eternal life.   *Nick Fawcett*

148   Loving God,
       you have come to us in Christ.
       So now we come to you,
       to offer our worship,
       to hear your word
       and to reflect on your love.
       Help us through all we share today
       to hear the story of Christmas speaking to us as though for
       the first time.
       May familiar and well-loved words take on new meaning,
       so that we may share the elation of Mary,
       the excitement felt by the shepherds,
       and the wonder experienced by the wise men.
       May what was news of great joy for them,
       bring joy likewise to us,
       this and every day,
       through Jesus Christ our Lord.   *Nick Fawcett*

149   Sovereign God,
       with Mary and Joseph gazing into the manger,
       with shepherds hurrying to and from the stable,
       with angels praising you on high,
       with wise men kneeling before the Christ child,
       and with generations across the years
       who have known and loved your Son,
       experiencing his presence in their lives,
       so now we join to marvel and celebrate,

145   Lord, as we remember the shepherds in the hills above
Bethlehem,
    open our eyes to your glory,
    open our ears to the songs of angels,
    grant to us the joy of the shepherds,
    that we may come to your presence,
    bow before you in love and adoration,
    and go on our way rejoicing.
    Through him who shared in our humanity,
    even Jesus Christ, our Lord.   *David Adam*

146   Sovereign God,
    we can never repay your goodness
    and never fully express our thanks,
    but we bring you again today our praise and worship,
    offered in the name of Jesus.
    Like the choir of angels on the night of his birth,
    we sing in adoration.
    Like the shepherds,
    returning from the manger,
    we give you praise for everything we have experienced.
    Like the magi,
    kneeling in wonder,
    we bring you our homage as a token of our love
    and a sign of our commitment.
    All we think, say, do and are
    we bring to you in reverent praise and joyful celebration,
    in the name of Christ.   *Nick Fawcett*

147   Loving God,
    we come today to remember with gratitude
    the birth of your Son.
    We remember how prophets foretold his coming,
    and how those words were wonderfully fulfilled in
Bethlehem.
    We remember how you needed Mary to bring him into
the world,
    and how she willingly allowed you to work through her.
    We remember how shepherds heard the good news,
    and how, having seen the truth of it for themselves,

and into our lives.
Let us enjoy your presence with us,
and the love you offer to us in Jesus our Lord.   *David Adam*

141   May the humility of the shepherds,
the perseverance of the wise men,
the joy of the angels,
be God's gifts to us and to people everywhere
this Christmas time.
And may the blessing of the Christ child
be upon us always.   *David Adam*

142   We ask your blessing
upon all who do not celebrate this Christmas.
We remember all who will be homeless or lonely
and all who are poor or deeply in debt.
We pray that our homes
may be places of love and peace
where you, Christ, are welcome.
May we know that in the coming of others to us
you also come and seek our love.   *David Adam*

143   We give thanks for our homes
and the friends with whom we will celebrate
this Christmas.
We remember absent friends and loved ones.
We remember all who are lonely
or feel rejected at this time.   *David Adam*

144   Holy Jesus, Son of God,
as we long to hear the songs of the angels,
may we keep our eyes and hearts fixed on your coming.
As we travel with the shepherds to Bethlehem,
may we bow before your beauty and your majesty.
When we return to our homes, fill our days with your glory,
that we may rejoice in your love and abiding presence,
Jesus Christ, our Saviour and our God.   *David Adam*

135   Jesus Christ, you have come
      to lift us into the fullness of your kingdom.
      You, dear Lord, have become human
      that we may share in your divinity.
      You have come to live among us
      that we may be your friends.
      We give you thanks for Christmas,
      for the gift of your presence and yourself.   *David Adam*

136   Every day can be a Christmas day,
      for the Lord comes to us as he came to Bethlehem.
      He seeks to be born in us,
      he wants us to come to him like the shepherds,
      he wants to live in and work through us,
      he comes eternally and seeks room in our lives,
      for the Lord comes to us as he came to Bethlehem.
                                David Adam

137   We give thanks that our Lord
      was born into an ordinary family
      and lived in an ordinary home.
      We ask your blessing
      upon all our loved ones and friends this Christmas:
      may we know your presence in our joys and celebrations.
      We remember all who have to spend this Christmas
      away from their homes and loved ones.   *David Adam*

138   Lord Jesus, you have come among us,
      to share in our lives and to let us share in yours.
      As you give yourself to us today,
      help us to give ourselves to you.   *David Adam*

139   We give thanks for all who celebrate Christmas,
      all who are worshipping in churches and in their homes,
      all who acknowledge Jesus in their midst.   *David Adam*

140   Father, we rejoice and sing,
      for you love us with a great love.
      We give thanks to you
      for the coming of our Lord Jesus Christ into our world

Christmas

133 God be with us on our journey towards Christmas.
Help us to go deeper into what is real
until we are brought to the wonder of your incarnation.
Dear Son of God, you took flesh to redeem us.
Forgive our hardness.
Dear Son of Mary,
with sacrifice of love you came to us.
Forgive our selfishness.   *Ray Simpson*

134 With Abraham and Moses,
waiting to be led to a place of promise,
we wait.
With Amos and Hosea, Isaiah, Micah,
and all the prophets believing
that you are a God of justice,
we wait.
With Paul and Silas,
and all God's people imprisoned and persecuted
for acting on their faith,
we wait.
With Naaman and Jairus,
Bartimaeus and the Syro-Phoenician woman,
longing for an end to pain and rejection,
we wait.
With Zaccheus in his tree
and the Samaritan widow at the well,
keen to be liberated from a half-life,
we wait.
With Sarah and Hannah, Elizabeth and Mary,
looking forward to new life and new beginnings,
we wait.
With Jesus in the desert,
and in the garden because he asks us to,
we wait.

Based on a prayer of The Wild Goose Resources Group

Ray Simpson

Come to them, Lord Jesus.
Desire of every nation,
we bring to you those who are exploring,
but who do not know what they search for.
Come to them, Lord Jesus.   *Ray Simpson*

130   Lord, you keep us waiting for signs of hope.
You keep us looking for ways in which you come.
The pain of the world, the anguish of the people
cry out to you.
Come, Lord Jesus, come.   *Ray Simpson*

131   Son of the prophets, on our longings
let your light shine.
Son of Mary, on our littleness
let your light shine.
Son of Eternity, on our lying down
let your light shine.   *Ray Simpson*

132   We wait in the darkness, expectantly, longingly;
come, O God Most High.
In the darkness we can see the splendour of the universe –
blankets of stars, the solitary glowing of the planets.
Come, O God Most High.
In the darkness of the womb mortals are nurtured
and the Christ child was made ready
for the journey into light.
Come, O God Most High.
In the darkness the wise three
found the star that led them to you.
Come, O God Most High.
In the darkness of dreams
you spoke to Joseph and the wise ones
and you speak still to us.
Come, O God Most High.
In the darkness of despair and distress
we watch for a sign of hope from the Light of lights.
Come, O God Most High.

Based on a Maori prayer from New Zealand   *Ray Simpson*

and root them in realities that nothing can destroy.
Key to Destiny,
unlock our potential
and our capacity to befriend and serve others,
that we may be mentors and soul friends
amid a needy people.
Light-bringer,
illumine places of darkness, despair and disease.
True Fulfiller of Desire, harness our deepest longings
to your infinite purpose of love.
God with us – the Presence that cannot be taken from us –
may we live with you and may you live in us for ever.

Ray Simpson

127 Great Spirit, swirling in the elements,
you brought to birth a world.
Mighty Father, swirling in the elements,
you brought to birth a Son.
Eternal Christ, swirling in the elements,
you stride towards us now.
Glory to God in the highest. *Ray Simpson*

128 You are holy, you are whole.
Let Earth give praise from pole to pole.
You are coming, coming here
to bring your hard-pressed people cheer;
bringing to them human birth
born of heaven, born of Earth;
bringing to them bread and wine,
giving hope of life divine.
You are coming, you are whole –
let Earth give praise from pole to pole. *Ray Simpson*

129 Desire of every nation,
we bring to you those who are empty
and who long to find meaning.
Come to them, Lord Jesus.
Desire of every nation,
we bring to you those who are overlooked
and who long to know their worth.

but our wholehearted adoration and joyful thanksgiving.
We would bring you our lives –
not just token deeds or outward show,
but hearts consecrated to your service,
embodying your love for all,
your care and compassion for everything you have made.
Receive, then, this time set aside for you
as a small yet sincere way of acknowledging your goodness,
and through it equip us to live as your people
this and every day.   *Nick Fawcett*

78   Living God,
       we do not understand all your ways or know all your
       thoughts.
       There is so much in our lives that troubles and confuses us –
       so much hurt and pain we cannot begin to make sense of.
       Yet we know that in Jesus you have shared our humanity,
       experiencing not just the good in it but the bad.
       You understand what it means to be hurt,
       to endure suffering,
       to face even death itself.
       As well as our joys you have shared our sorrows.
       Living God,
       we thank you for the assurance this gives us –
       that whatever we face you will be with us in it. *Nick Fawcett*

Throughout Advent

79   Heavenly Father,
       during this Advent season
       we thank you for feeding us
       in body, mind and spirit.   *Susan Sayers*

80   The world moves round into the light of the day
       and we thank you, Father, that we are alive in it.
       In this Advent season of watching and waiting,
       keep us attentive to you, throughout the day,
       ready to listen, ready to learn and ready to love. *Susan Sayers*

81   Another Advent has begun.
Lord our God,
lead us in the way of truth and love,
kindness and mercy.
As we get ready for Christmas,
may we learn more about loving you
and loving one another.
Give us courage to keep asking
the big questions about life and death,
knowing that you are in our past, our present and
all our future.
You know us completely and you love us completely.
Thank you, Lord God, for making us,
and for coming to be born among us as a baby.
May we worship you with our whole lives.   *Susan Sayers*

82   In this dark time of the year
we are reminded of our need for light.
Prepare our hearts to hold more love,
so that the world's darkness may grow less
and the light of love shine brighter.   *Susan Sayers*

83   Where we are cold and in darkness
warm and brighten us.
Where we are forgetful of our calling
remind and refresh us.
Where we have lost hope
revive and restore us.
Where we have lost our way
find us and set us once again
on the path of life.   *Susan Sayers*

84   Through the generations
your people waited in hope and expectation.
Now in the darkness of this Advent night
we relive that waiting with them,
relive that small bright hope
as it brightens into the full glory
'as of the only begotten of the Father –
full of grace and truth'.
Amen. Come, Lord Jesus!   *Susan Sayers*

85   Lord, this Advent, grant us humility
to step out of the driving seat
in the way we live,
so that we honour the other
in each conversation,
listening rather than imposing
our own ideas,
however cleverly and subtly we
have learnt to do this undetected. *Susan Sayers*

86   As we battle with the inevitable rush up to Christmas,
grant us a less wasteful approach
to the way we shop and manage our living,
for a deeper concern
for living with a small footprint on the planet
and for a greater appreciation
of the recycled gifts we receive,
like clean water and reflected moonlight. *Susan Sayers*

87   As we prepare ourselves
for the time when Christ comes again in glory,
we pray for the grace and honesty
to see what needs transforming in our lives as individuals
and as members of the Church of God.
May we all be given a new enthusiasm
for walking God's way, clothed in the armour of light.

Susan Sayers

88   Lord, in our constantly changing world,
with its shifting values and fragile ecological balance,
root us deeply in your unchanging nature
of mercy, goodness, faithfulness and love.
Awaken us to expect you with joy;
we give you thanks for your tender parenting
and your unfailing patience with us. *Susan Sayers*

89   Lord, we long for your kingdom
to come in our world,
and to flood with truth and love
the disillusion, hopelessness and terror

which traps the human spirit
and chokes its potential joy.
Thank you, Lord of hope,
for the way you surprise us with joy,
and show us the extraordinary and the wonderful
in the ordinary things of life. *Susan Sayers*

90   God of warmth and brightness,
we praise you for all our many blessings,
and above all for coming to save us and set us free.

Susan Sayers

91   Lord of heaven, we thank you
for your faithful promise to us,
fulfilled in the coming of Jesus.
We welcome his kingship in our lives. *Susan Sayers*

92   Holy God, just as we are we come to you,
and ask for your kingdom to come in us
and in this place;
increase our faith and our love for you,
so that we may become the lights in darkness
that we are called to be. *Susan Sayers*

93   As followers of the living Christ,
we praise you for the prophecies fulfilled,
the promises honoured and the victory over evil
gloriously accomplished in him
to fill our lives with hope. *Susan Sayers*

94   Lord of heaven, may we be
quiet enough to hear your voice,
humble enough to move your way,
and excited enough to spread the good news. *Susan Sayers*

95   Lord of heaven, grant us patience and courage
when our waiting seems long and painful;
give us assurance of your presence. *Susan Sayers*

96 As we think about the fulfilment of all things today,
    we speak with you, Lord, the God of our making.
    We pray that we will all be ready
    to meet you face to face,
    whenever that will be.   *Susan Sayers*

97 We know that you, Lord, are here with us,
    and hear what is in our thoughts and in our hearts.
    We ask for a real longing for you in our lives;
    a longing that is not satisfied by anything else. *Susan Sayers*

98 Father, we want to be ready to receive you.
    Take us as we are and cultivate in us
    a heart that longs for you and worships you
    above and beyond everything else.   *Susan Sayers*

99 As we share in Mary and Elizabeth's joy
    at the coming of our Saviour,
    we quieten and still ourselves
    in the presence of you, God.
    Heavenly Father, we can only marvel
    at the way you are happy to work with us.
    We want you to know
    that we are willing to be used.   *Susan Sayers*

100 As we approach the festival of Christmas,
    we praise and thank you for the full provision
    you have given us
    through the coming of Jesus.   *Susan Sayers*

101 To the tune of 'See saw, Marjorie Daw':
    Jesus, Jesus,
    coming to earth as a baby,
    Jesus, Jesus,
    coming to earth as a baby.   *Susan Sayers*

102   To the tune from Beethoven's Pastoral Symphony,
'Thanksgiving after the storm':
God comes to save us,
he comes to set us free,
he loves us, he loves us,
for all eternity.   *Susan Sayers*

103   To the tune of Eastenders:
Candle burning in the night,
showing us the light
of Jesus our Saviour.
Candle burning in the night,
tell us of the Light
which shines in our world with love.   *Susan Sayers*

104   To the tune of 'Frère Jacques':
Advent candles, Advent candles,
burning bright, burning bright,
lighting up our darkness, lighting up our darkness
with God's light, with God's light.   *Susan Sayers*

105   Dear God,
the world is full of your love. (trace big circle)
Help us to listen out for it. (cup ears)
Help us to watch out for it. (shade eyes and look around)
Thank you for all the goodness and love
that we can hear and see.   *Susan Sayers*

106   As we prepare ourselves
for the time when Christ comes again in glory,
we pray for the grace and honesty
to see what needs transforming
in our lives as individuals
and as members of the Church of God.   *Susan Sayers*

107   Lord, help us to see
the signs of your love today
in the world around us
and in the people we meet.

Train us to be ready to see you
and recognise you
when you come in glory.   *Susan Sayers*

108   Lord our God,
make us watchful and keep us faithful
as we wait for the coming of your Son our Lord;
that, when he appears,
he may not find us sleeping in sin
but active in his service
and joyful in his praise.   *Susan Sayers*

109   Heavenly Father,
we thank you for helping us
to get ourselves ready to receive you.   *Susan Sayers*

110   Dear Jesus,
when I open today's window
in my Advent calendar
I remember the present
I am getting ready to give you.
Please help me to do it well.   *Susan Sayers*

111   Lord God,
help us to get ourselves ready
to welcome you
into our lives.   *Susan Sayers*

112   Lord, awaken us to expect you with joy;
we give you thanks for your tender parenting
and your unfailing patience with us.   *Susan Sayers*

113   Lord,
help me
to recognise you today.   *Susan Sayers*

114   Lord Jesus Christ,
you have no body on earth but ours,
no hands but ours,
no feet but ours.

Ours are the eyes through which
your compassion must look out on the world.
Ours are the feet by which
you may still go about doing good.
Ours are the hands with which
you bless people now.
Bless our minds and bodies,
that we may be a blessing to others.

Based on a prayer of St Teresa of Avila   *Susan Sayers*

115   Calm us to wait for the gift of Christ.
      Cleanse us to prepare the way for Christ.
      Teach us to contemplate the wonder of Christ.
      Anoint us to bear the life of Christ.   *Ray Simpson*

116   Christ, wake us to your summons, urgent in our midst,
      to truth we cannot hide from – your power alone will last.
      The worlds that now so scorn you will vanish like a dream.
      When you take back your own; all good will be one stream.

      Based on a prayer of George McLeod   *Ray Simpson*

117   In the wasteland may the Glory shine.
      In the land of the lost may the King make his home.

                                                    Ray Simpson

118   All-knowing God,
      parents-in-God picture and pattern your ways;
      forgive us for following idols and illusions.
      All-seeing God,
      prophets shine like candles in the night;
      forgive us for staying in the dark.
      All-holy God,
      front runners like John clear obstacles from your path;
      forgive us for blocking your way.
      All-giving God,
      people like Mary offered their all as bearers of your life;
      help us to be bearers of your life.   *Ray Simpson*

119   Lord, though we may laugh
at failed end-of-world predictions,
may we live this day
as if you will come
and find us doing our duty with joy,
alert and ready to meet you.   *Ray Simpson*

120   Help us to prepare a way for you:
by our thoughtfulness towards others;
by our care in little things;
by our upholding of the oppressed.   *Ray Simpson*

121   Help us to prepare a way for you:
by our thoughtfulness towards creatures;
by our care of crops and kitchens;
by our upholding of creation.   *Ray Simpson*

122   The Earth is becoming a wasteland:
Breath of the Most High, come and renew it.
Humanity is becoming a battleground:
Child of Peace, come and unite it.
Society is becoming a playground:
Key of Destiny, open doors to our true path.
The world is becoming a no-man's-land:
God with us, come and make your home here. *Ray Simpson*

123   Christ, Light of the world,
meet us in our place of darkness.
Christ, Light of the world,
meet us in our place of longing.
Christ, Light of the world,
meet us in our place of working.   *Ray Simpson*

124   Among the hungry,
among the homeless,
among the friendless,
come to make things new.
Among the powerful,
among the spoilt,

among the crooked,
come to make things new.
In halls of fame,
in corridors of power,
in forgotten places,
come to make things new.
With piercing eyes,
with tender touch,
with cleansing love,
come to make things new.   *Ray Simpson*

125   Come to us, Wisdom,
      moving in the flux and flow of the cosmos
      to bring worlds into being.
      Come to us, Wisdom,
      permeating all creation,
      the life of soil and seed and seasons.
      Come to us, Wisdom,
      shaping nations and ensouling peoples.
      Come to us, Wisdom,
      encompassing the mysteries of the unseen world
      and the mysteries of the soul.
      Come to us, Wisdom,
      the seeing eye of art and science,
      the ear of all that breathes.
      Come to us, Wisdom,
      the light of our darkness,
      the reconciler of that which is divided.
      Come to us, Wisdom,
      the weaver of Earth's destiny,
      the completer of our call.   *Ray Simpson*

126   Wisdom, permeating creation and informing all peoples,
      come and bring us the mind of God.
      Shaper of peoples,
      who through Moses
      gave guidance that would make a people great,
      guide us into the ways of true greatness.
      Bedrock, Sign of community,
      come to places of instability